# VEILED
# CONFESSIONS

## "Drawing Heart's Strings"

Khyati Swain

BookLeaf Publishing

India | USA | UK

# Dedication

This book is dedicated to every **raw**, **imperfect** human on this planet—those who feel deeply, who love and hurt, who laugh and cry, who wonder and wander. May these poems remind you that every emotion is a part of **your** truth, a piece of the beautiful complexity that makes us all **human**. Through joy, pain, or silence, we are all connected by the feelings that shape our lives.

# Preface

Have you ever felt a feeling so deep that the world seems to slip through your fingers like grains of sand? That's exactly why I wrote this book. In these pages, you'll find yourself reflected in *21 different emotional mirrors* – each one capturing a unique shade of what it means to be *human*.

You know those moments when your heart feels too full or too empty? When joy bottles you up or sadness weighs heavy like anchor? Yeah, those feelings – ***all of them*** – they're here.

# Acknowledgements

*"With heartfelt gratitude to everyone who has contributed to my journey of emotions..."*

# 1. DEJECTION

Wandering thoughts, wondering hearts,
Tiredness engulfed within, will I ever fit in?
Thrown around, played with like darts,
Shadowed in every aspect, shot like a pin.

Pushed beside, never in anyone's polaroids,
Bottled sayings, always a backup plan,
Dripping in favours, swimming into voids,
Never admired, always a fan.

Trying my best to be **one of them,** but I'm not even **one,**
Even the brightest stars burn they say, am I even a star?
Everyone's but no one's,
Looking at **their** table from afar.

Tried to laugh, but my voice felt thin,
Like an echo of someone they all forget.
Tried to belong, but I'm still wearing this skin,
Tired of being here, yet too scared to leave it just yet.

Hands that held promises, now just hold the air,
No one's eyes to catch, no words to spare.
I've spoken my truths, but they've all slipped through,
Like water through fingers, slipping from view.

Worn-out shoes from chasing their pace,
Yet, no one notices the effort I waste.
I give and I give, but my hands come back bare,
Like the rest of them, I'm never quite there.

A shadow I stand, dimmed by their light,
Trying to shine, but always out of sight.
I've heard their laughter, felt the divide,
Wondered how it feels to have a place, a side.

They say "you belong," but it never feels true,
Like a room full of voices, but none calling you.
I'm stretched out, bending to fit what's not me,
Just a ripple in a world that will never set me free.

# 2. ENVY

Your eyes, your nose, your lips—how they shine,
Like a star that gets all the love, all the time.
You move through life with effortless grace,
While I'm here, stuck in your shadow, in this empty
space.

I watch as they all flock to you,
Like moths to a flame, I'm just... passing through.
You don't even notice, don't even see,
The way I burn with envy just to be *you*, to be free.

Your laugh, that perfect sound,
Hissing through my grounded frowns.
But here I am, an echo, a sigh,
Watching you soar as I crawl and cry.

Envy claws, but it doesn't let go,
Because no matter how I try, I can never grow.
Yet in my heart, a bitter truth lies—
The more I envy, the more I disguise.

For in wanting you, I lose my own face,
Chasing your shadow, I'm losing my place.
Perhaps, one day, I'll learn to see
That the life I want is the one that's free,

No more will I chase what was never mine,
But rather, I'll grow where my roots intertwine.
In the soil of my own self, I'll begin to sow,
For peace blooms only when you let envy go.

# 3. NOSTALGIA

I find myself lost in a shadowed lane,
Where echoes of laughter still call my name.
The air is thick with days long gone,
And in the stillness, I linger on.

I remember the way the light would fall,
Soft and warm, like a lover's call,
The sound of your voice, clear and near,
Now only a murmur I barely hear.

I reach for those moments, a trembling hand,
Trying to hold what slipped like sand.
The world was wide, our hearts were free,
But time, it takes, and swallows the sea.

I see it now in the corner of my mind,
A place where I left so much behind,
And though I know it's all been lost,
I keep chasing it, no matter the cost.

I still feel you there, like the morning dew,
A part of me that I once knew.
But in the silence, I only find
The echo of what we left soo far behind.

Perhaps, I'll never grasp what's gone,
But in the dark, I'll keep moving on.
For in each step, I find a trace,
Of what once was, and still has grace.

So I keep chasing, through the night,
The fleeting glow of what felt right.
For though the past may slip and slide,
In my heart, it's where I still reside.

# 4. ANEMOIA

In quiet corners of my mind I stray,
Through sepia haze where fleeting shadows play,
Where echoes of soft laughter, sweet and light,
Float like petals caught in soft moonlight.

I feel the weight of years I've never known,
A longing for a past I call my own,
Corsets, florals, cigars in smoky air,
A time I've never touched but feel aware.

The streets are paved with faces I can't name,
In shades of grey, they pass me all the same,
Each smile a thread in woven tapestry,
Each sigh a murmur of some lost decree.

I chase the ghosts of yesterdays undone,
Through alleys brushed with hues of setting sun,
Where whispered tales of lives once lived unfold,
And all the quiet stories still are told.

A traveler I am, in dreams I roam,
In lands of past, I search for a lost home,
In every turn, I sense a world I've known,
Yet in my hands, its history is shown.

I wear the weight of time unclaimed, unseen,
As though I've walked through lives that might have
been,
Each moment calls, yet all remain a blur—
A bittersweet, unspoken time's allure.

# 5. ONISM

I stand before the screen,
a map of places I will never know,
each name blinking like a distant heartbeat,
flickering, fading, forgotten.

There's a city I'll never step in,
a sunrise I'll never see,
a language I'll never learn,
a wall I'll never touch.

I am here,
just here,
in this moment,
as the world spins out of reach.

I trace the letters of places I can't pronounce,
imagine their streets, their air,
the weight of their histories I will never carry—
I feel the ache of what I cannot grasp.

It's as if I'm standing on the edge of something vast,
a map sprawled out across the world,
and I am stuck at the point
marked with an arrow,
tiny, insignificant, still.

I'll never walk down that road,
never taste the salt on that breeze,
never feel the pulse of that city at night.
And the arrow spins, and I'm here—
always here,
staring at the screen,
at what could have been.

# 6. GUILT

A shadow clinging, dark and deep,
Where secrets stir and memories sleep.
A whisper haunting, soft and low,
A seed of sorrow, starts to grow.

It gnaws within, a constant ache,
A promised consequence, you cannot shake.
A heavy cloak, you're forced to wear,
A silent judgment, beyond compare.

It twists the truth, distorts the sight,
And shrouds the soul in endless night.
A phantom echo of what's done,
A battle fought, and never won.

Can absolution ease the pain?
Can righting wrongs break guilt's harsh chain?
Perhaps forgiveness, hard to find,
Can liberate the captive mind.

But until then, the shadow stays,
A constant reminder of bygone days.
Guilt's bitter lesson, learned in strife,
A heavy burden, borne through life.

# 7. SCABULOUS

A scar upon my skin, a story told,
A mark of strength, though the years grow cold.
Not from a fight, but from days I stayed,
When life was dark, and I felt betrayed.

It's my autograph, signed with grace,
A pact with the world I cannot erase.
In every line, a whisper speaks,
Of times I fell, of times I peaked.

The world, though wild, still called my name,
And I responded, through grief and flame.
This scar is proof I chose to stay,
Even when shadows led me astray.

A scar that tells of battles won,
Though none were fought beneath the sun.
It's not a mark of weakness, no,
But of a spirit that refuses to go.

A signature from life's cruel hand,
But in its wake, I chose to stand.
The scar is mine, an emblem proud,
Of resilience spoken, though not aloud.

And though I may not always fight,
The scar reminds me of my might.
For I have danced with the world's rough ways,
And still, I rise to greet the days.

# 8. ALTSCHMERZ

A circle worn, a path well-tread,
Where old flaws and fears have bled.
The same old ache, the same old strain,
A song replayed in endless rain.

Altschmerz, it whispers soft and deep,
In quiet moments when we sleep.
The taste of old regret, gone cold,
A story that was once so bold.

Familiar pains, they reappear,
Tired whispers of ancient fear.
Gnawing at the edges of the mind,
Worn-out thoughts, no peace to find.

You chew on sorrow, stale and thin,
Yet still it lingers, wrapped within.
And when you've spat it all away,
You seek new wounds where shadows play.

In the backyard, a grave is found,
Where buried hurts still make a sound.
You dig for sorrow, fresh and pure,
Chasing ghosts, but never sure.

So on you wander, restless, still,
With nothing new but the same old chill.
Altschmerz, a quiet, weary friend,
Who promises no start or end.

# 9. CRUSHING

In the hallways, where we pass,
A stolen glance, a moment's class.
Your smile, a spark I can't ignore,
A secret crush I can't ignore.

I watch you laugh, so unaware,
Of the feelings hanging in the air.
My heart beats fast, but lips stay sealed,
A silent love that's never revealed.

From best friends to something more,
We talk, we laugh, but I still adore
The quiet way you make me see
The world, a place where you and me
Could just be.

We're opposites, yet we connect,
A bond I never thought we'd get.
The moments stolen in the halls,
The secret dates behind the walls.

But maybe, love's not meant to stay,
In schoolyard dreams, where hearts must sway,
From friends to lovers, and then apart,
A lesson learned in the tender heart.

So, I'll hold on to what we had,
The highs, the lows, the good, the bad.
In this school romance, sweet yet brief,
We wrote our story, shared belief.

And though the years may pull us far,
We'll always keep that secret star—
The one we shared when we were young,
A whispered song, a love unsung.

# 10. OCCHIOLISM

In the hush of my mind, I glimpse the world,
A vast, uncharted ocean, beyond all reach,
My thoughts, like grains of sand, are tossed and swirled,
Each moment whispers that I cannot teach.

I stand, a speck, beneath the endless sky,
A single story, told in whispered air,
An epic written just before I die,
Yet pales in contrast to what's unfolding there.

The past, a flicker in the flame of time,
The future waits behind an iron door.
What can I know, but feel the endless climb,
When others live a thousand lives, or more?

Awake, I tremble at my tiny view,
A world so grand, yet distant—who can say?
Perhaps my tale, though dear, is born askew,
A fleeting echo, drifting far away.

So here I stand, with nothing left to prove,
Just one brief glimpse, a heart unsure to move.

# 11. LIBEROSIS

Liberosis, a dance with air,
A soft surrender, free from care.
The weightless pull, the gentle drift,
No more to grasp, no need to lift.

A life held lightly, like a ball,
In fleeting touches, free for all.
We juggle moments, let them slip,
Between our palms, we let them flip.

No fear of loss, no heavy clutch,
Just playful hands, not needing much.
It bounces here, it soars up high,
Untethered, like the open sky.

We play with time, we let it go,
Like waves that ebb, like winds that blow.
In trust, in joy, we take our chance,
To live, to love, in fleeting dance.

Liberosis, the art of light,
Letting go to take flight.
In the game of life, we rise and fall,
But hold it loosely, after all.

In the breeze, we find our way,
A dance that leads, but cannot stay.
With every step, a breath, a song,
We float through life, where we belong.

# 12. VEMÖDALEN

In the moment, I lift the lens,
Chasing light, the beauty bends,
A sunset bleeding into sky,
But thousands have captured this, and why?

The curve of land, the wave's soft fall,
The shimmer in a lover's call—
All this, already, etched and stored,
Echoes in a crowded hoard.

What once was new, now feels so worn,
A truth we've shared, too oft, reborn.
A hollow pulse beneath my touch,
That once held wonder, now too much.

I snap, and still the magic fades,
Drowned in the river of mirrored shades.
The wonder's lost, the moment sold,
A fleeting vision turned too bold.

And yet, I click again, once more,
Still chasing what is here before—
For even in the flood, the game,
A spark survives, untouched by fame.

# 13. NIGHTHAWK

It comes as the sky bleeds into dusk,
a shadow that slides through the crack of the door,
not in haste but with patient wings,
swaying softly on the edges of thought.

A task, forgotten, now dressed in midnight,
its weight lighter in the silence of hours,
but it circles, sharp-eyed,
hovering just beyond the glass of tomorrow.

You think you've outrun it,
pushed it to the back of your mind,
but it knows, always knows,
how to wait for you—slowly, quietly,
building a nest in the corners of your room.

While the moon hangs, indifferent,
your thoughts weave together like branches,
each worry a twig, a thread,
until they form a delicate cage

around your thoughts—
a bird, a beast, a keeper of dreams
that keeps you awake,
your coffee long gone,

but the nighthawk still there,
waiting for its turn.
Tomorrow, you promise,
but tonight, it pecks,
and you let it.

# 14. ETTERATH

The race is done, the battle's through,
The weight that crushed has now unglued,
A breath of peace, a sigh of light,
But something lingers in the night.

The mission's over, and I stand,
With empty hands and thoughts unplanned,
Relief, yes, but something's missing,
The rush, the drive—the pulse, now hissing.

Once I thrived on chaos' reign,
On plans, on lists, on dreams to gain.
Now stillness wraps its gentle hold,
Yet I feel a longing for the bold.

Is this the price of victory?
To let go of all that used to be,
To search for purpose in the quiet,
Where once there was a constant riot?

I've conquered, yes, but now what's left?
This space of calm, this gentle theft.
I long for structure, for the chase,
For mission's mark, for that old pace.

So, here I stand, in peace, in doubt,
No task to finish, no task to rout.
But maybe, just maybe, in the still,
There's room to breathe, to dream, to fill.

# 15. AMICY

In shadows, quiet whispers grow,
Where stories hide that none will know,
Behind the curtain, veiled and thin,
The tangled threads that weave within.

There are rooms you'll never see,
A web of words, a silent plea,
Back channels hum with secret sound,
Connections where the lost are found.

In corners dark, the past is kept,
The history of what was swept,
Affiliations, once so clear,
Now shrouded in a distant sphere.

You walk the streets, eyes wide and free,
But here, behind, there's mystery—
A dance of faces, names unseen,
The quiet power of what's between.

A second life, a secret flame,
A quiet call, no voice, no name—
And though you live, and laugh, and roam,
There's always more behind your home.

So wonder not at what you miss,
The silent truths, the hidden kiss,
For somewhere, in the folds of time,
The mystery is always mine.

# 16. WATASHIATO

I wonder, in the quiet hum,
Of passing days and moments numb,
What ripple from my fleeting touch,
Might have shaped a life so much.

A word I spoke, too soft, too light,
Perhaps it sparked a change that night,
A harmless jest, a smile so wide,
Did it steer someone to a side?

The paths we walk, so close, so far,
Yet never knowing where they are,
How many lives did I unknowingly bend,
And which ones I'll never comprehend?

For we are threads in unseen lace,
In lives we've touched, in time and space,
Though we may never know the trace,
The echoes linger, in their place.

How many hearts did we not see,
Shift course, grow bold, or simply flee?
The words once lost, the gestures slight,
Might hold a story, out of sight.

In silent wonder, I now reside,
Curious of the turns they've tried,
A fleeting act, a whispered word,
A change, in ways we've never heard.

# 17. ÉNOUEMENT

I stand on this quiet precipice,
A moment stretched between the now and then,
Where answers drift, like leaves in a breeze,
From futures wrapped in forgotten pens.

The weight of knowing pulls me back,
To days I thought I'd left behind,
To see my sister, grown and bold,
A stranger with a spark I once had found.

The faces of my friends fade slow,
Into the paths they've chosen well,
I wonder who they've turned into,
And what untold stories time will tell.

In this space, I yearn to shout,
To tell them all I now can see,
What choices come with hidden cost,
And when we lose, who we used to be.

Yet here I stand, with all my truth,
In a place where time slips like sand,
And some small part of me remains,
Back in the past, a waiting hand.

Waiting to hear the tales still untold,
To share the answers, sweet and bitter,
From this future I've learned to hold,
And the present, where I never quite fit her.

# 18. KENOPSIA

Kenopsia, the quiet's sting,
Where echoes once did brightly sing,
Now still, the halls hold silent screams,
Ghosts of lives in fractured dreams.

A school where laughter used to glide,
Now empty benches sit aside,
The air is thick with what's been lost,
In the hush, the price is cost.

Fairgrounds that once would hum with light,
Now swallow shadows in the night,
Twirling rides abandoned still,
A hollow wind runs through the chill.

A vacant office, desks askew,
No hands to type, no words to view,
The hum of phones, the rustling paper—
Faint whispers of a time much safer.

In every space, in every sigh,
A warmth is gone, a life gone by,
Kenopsia blooms in the vacant stare,
A world once full, now stripped bare.

It's the space where absence speaks,
A hollow call, an echo's peak,
The eerie glow of what's no more—
An emptiness we can't ignore.

# 19. ANTHRODYNIA

In the quiet of the world's cruel hum,
Where hearts bruise and the weary succumb,
There's a place untouched by all the scorn,
A place where joy is freshly born.

Exhausted, beaten by the weight of lies,
A soul surrenders to the truth in disguise,
And in the cracks of what once felt whole,
There blooms affection for a gentle soul.

Not the faces that judge or turn away,
But the kindness in the simplest display,
The unshamed dance of a laughing child,
The pure love of a pet, soft and wild.

How sweet the touch of things that just *are*,
Like the moon rising, a steady star.
When humans falter and their love feels thin,
These small joys remind me where to begin.

For in this tired world of endless pain,
It's the truth of joy that still remains—
A counter to the bitterness we carry,
A spark of light that makes hearts merry.

In anthrodynia, I find my grace,
In simple truth, I find my place.

# 20. XENO

A glance, a spark, a fleeting trace,
In crowded rooms, an empty space.
A nod, a smile, two hearts aligned,
In those brief seconds, souls entwined.

Strangers in a world so vast,
Whispering moments, shadows cast.
No words exchanged, yet there it lies—
A connection born with no goodbyes.

A laugh that ripples, soft and free,
Two lives adrift, yet momentarily,
Beneath the noise, a silent hum—
A tiny bond that says, "You're not numb."

In passing, fleeting as the wind,
A touch, a spark, a world pinned.
Small as xeno, yet still profound,
The quiet dance of souls unbound.

For though we part, and time moves on,
The echo lingers, soft, and strong.
And in the briefest, sweetest exchange,
Loneliness begins to rearrange.

# 21. HEARTWORM

It's that name that flashes on your screen,
A Snapchat ping you didn't ask for,
A story you didn't watch but still haunt,
A message unread, waiting,
Like the weight of something unfinished.

It's the late-night thoughts that slip through cracks,
Not loud, but constant,
Like an itch you scratch and scratch
But never quite heal.

You scroll through Instagram,
And there they are,
A selfie, a caption, a moment—
And just like that,
The past creeps back in,
With a warmth you didn't expect,
But somehow *feel.*

A friendship—no, something else—

That fizzled like fireworks at dawn,
And you thought you'd let it go.

But here you are,
Picking at the edges,
Wondering if it ever truly left.
There are days when you forget,
And the world feels light,

But then, a memory, a laugh, a touch—
And there it is again,
That knot in your chest,
That thing you didn't ask for,

But somehow can't shake.
It's unfinished,
Not in a way that makes sense,
But in a way that echoes.

A campsite abandoned,
Embers still faintly glowing,
Just enough to set the trees alight
If you dared to step back in.

And you want to walk away,
Tell yourself it's over,
That the forest's been burned and regrown.

But something about the heat
Is too familiar to ignore.

43